HeartBeats

Anthology of Poetry

Heart Beats

Heart Beats

Anthology of Poetry

Lisa Tomey, Editor & Contributing Author

Prolific Pulse

Published by Prolific Pulse Press LLC

Raleigh NC

Copyright © Heart Beats Edited by Lisa Tomey

March 2021

All Rights Reserved, worldwide. No part of this publication may be reproduced, stored in, or introduced into a retrieval system, or transmitted in any form or by any means (electronic, mechanical, photocopying, recording, or otherwise) without prior written permission, except in the case of brief quotations embodied in critical articles and reviews. All trademarks used herein are the property of their respective owners. All rights revert to the contributing poets.

Library of Congress Control Number: 2021903453

ISBN 978-1-7365620-0-0

Cover Art by: Kay Doiron

thesweetestlittlepea@gmail.com

DEDICATION

To the wonderful poets who came forward with such beautiful works. The process of making choices was most difficult, but I believe we have here a wonderful collection. I am so proud to see this come into a reality, as it has been a dream to see poets come together and share about what makes their heart—beat, what makes them happy.

Thank you to all who contributed to this anthology. It truly makes my heart beat.

Heart Beats

ACKNOWLEDGEMENTS

Arlene S. Bice: "The Cart Lady" - Previously published in *Simply Put.*

Karla Linn Merrifield: "Swamp Psalm of the Water Sprite" Previously published in *Plum Tree Tavern,* October 2015; reprinted in *The Best of Plum Tree Tavern,* May 2016.

Karol Nielsen: "Instagram" and "Listener" Previously published in *Otherwise Engaged, A Literature and Arts Journal, Volume 6* Winter 2020.

Nayanjyoti Baruah: "Happiness" Previously published in *Rasa Literary Review,* India 2020.

Marjorie Maddox: "Transplanted" Previously published in *Ars Medica* and forthcoming in *Heart Speaks, Is Spoken For* (Shanti Arts, 2021);

"Ode to Almost Silence" Previously published in *The Grotto*;

"Inside" Previously published in *The Mom Egg Review* and forthcoming in *Begin with a Question* (Paraclete Press, 2021)

Heart Beats

TABLE OF CONTENTS

1	Arlene Bice
7	Aruna Gurumurthy
10	Barbara Truncellito
15	Bartholomew Barker
19	Brian Hayes
26	Bruce McRae
28	Carrie Levine
31	Ceinwen E Cariad Haydon
35	Chanah Wizenberg
44	Chyrel J. Jackson
51	Colin James
54	Danielle Martin
57	Dorothy La Motta
62	Elizabeth O. Ogunmode
65	Frank Hubeny
68	Ivor Steven
73	Jaya Avendel
77	JeanMarie Olivieri
80	Jill Sharon Kimmelman
84	Joan McNerney
90	John Lambremont, Sr.
95	Jose Castilleja
100	Joyce Lindenmuth

106	Karla Linn Merrifield
110	Karol Nielsen
113	Kathy Bryant
118	Katie Jenkins
123	Krzystzof Dabrowski
125	Lauren Clemmons
131	LaVan Robinson
135	Leslie Chartier
141	Lucy Brummett
145	marisela brazfield
147	Marjorie Maddox
153	Maya Dykstra
158	Michael Murdoch
162	Nayanjyoti Baruah
167	Norbert Gora
169	Peniel Gifted
172	Richard O. Ogunmode
175	Richard Oyama
179	Ronda Smith
181	Sarfraz Ahmed
185	Sheila DC Robertson
191	Sreekala P. Vijayan
193	Susi Bocks
197	Vandana Sudheesh
199	Lisa Tomey

INTRODUCTION

Heart Beats is an anthology of poetry about the various aspects of what makes us tick or makes a heart beat. This is about love, life, happiness, anything that makes life more joyful or tolerable.

Let's face it. These are tough times and there have been many events in 2020 which have many of us shaking our heads. People who were once friends have gone their separate ways. Some are soul searching, examining life more closely as time has leant more for this.

Heart Beats is about working through and maybe even overcoming these challenges. It is about what brings smiles to our faces or, at least, in our hearts. Heart Beats is about life, ups and down and in-betweens and how different points of view merge into one beautiful collection of poetic works.

Inviting poets from the world to participate, made this project even more meaningful. We are a world of people and the poetry community has become more culturally diverse. This is largely due to the pandemic as people are interacting virtually more than before.

What has now become a worn-out cliché "It Takes a Village" is still true. It took a virtual village of poets to make this anthology happen. When you enter this village, which is now a book, perhaps visit each author's poem as a door to their village domain. If you could sit with that poet and share a cuppa, what would you talk to them about? What common bond would you have in order to stir up your heart beats?

Heart Beats

Arlene S. Bice

arlene s bice, author, speaker, educator, and editor, is a member of TAF, IWWG and founding member of Warren Artists Market. She is the recipient of the Florence Poets Society Poet of Distinction Award.

Website: arlenebice.com

A Gift to Remember

You came to me that evening
trudging in a thick snowstorm
to dine, just us two, like music
we danced softly, warm in the night
candles glowed and so did we.

I remember the sight of you
in your heavy, winter overcoat
snow glistening silver in your hair
eyes sparkly as your coat opened
to uncover a single red rose of love.

If I were to remember one gift
of many gifts you gave to me
it would be that one red rose,
it wrapped around my heart
capturing me for you alone.

a gift to remember…

Heart Beats

Valentine's Day 1997

my husband had passed away
'twas the first winter of being alone,
approaching quickly was Valentine's Day

i sold a lot of chocolates
loving cards flew off the shelf
jewelry of sparkling stones, i wrapped myself

lovely gift baskets and deliveries kept me busy
no time to think or feel, business was a tizzy
at the end of the day as i was about to flop
the door opened jangly before i closed the shop

ahoy! a delivery for me! a mistake, i began to shout
"no, no!" the delivery man said; a surprise turnabout

my love was gone for good, no one could fill his shoes
so, what was this package who would so choose
to send a gift on this day

Heart Beats

thoughtful antique sellers, neighbors became so dear
Pete and Tom were the fellers; sent their love to me
with a tall hot air balloon, its basket filled with beauty

instead of holding sadness, or doom and gloom that day
joy overflowed my heart, a choice i gladly say
letting deep sadness go adrift, a bit of comfort in a gift.

It is all about love . . . and choice.

The Cart Lady

"Coffee or tea?
regular or decaf?
cream & sugar?
real sugar or the other?
A couple of donut holes?
two? I only give two or else
I wouldn't make it around the
bend-they'd all be gone for sure"

She added a bit of sunshine
in this waiting room
at Duke Eye Clinic
raising heads up
out of books,
crosswords
papers

with a
yes, no,
thank you
or a comment
to coax a laugh from her
and her laugh came easily

she was a morning blessing
dressed in Duke blue
eyes sparkled behind
her glasses, to
match her

silver-top head
like a crown
deserved
as I waited.

Aruna Gurumurthy

Aruna Gurumurthy is an American author, creative thinker, and poet. Since her childhood in Mumbai, India, she has embarked on a journey of creative exploration and, within her short prose poems, sestinas, and free verse, tries to capture the beauty and art in the world.

Gurumurthy has published seven books of poetry, essays and observations, *Diya: A Megawatt Approach to Change* (2015), *Spark* (2016), *A Beginning to the End* (2017), *Buddha In the Brain* (2018), *Puppet Dolls* (2018) and *Simplicity Beckons* (2019), *and Down the Grassy Aisles*, Kelsey Books (2020) She is published in regional anthologies, *Heron Clan V* (2018) & *VI* (2019) (Katherine James Books), *What it is to Be A Woman* and several journals. She resides with her family in Chapel Hill, NC.

A New Country

Auburn leaves of the sycamore tree quiver down the window, scatter and settle on the deck of the treehouse. Six years old, she cups those bits of splendor in her tiny palms and lays them down. The swerving winds gently whisk the leaves away. We sweep the beauties, bring them back to tranquility, weave them with burlap string creating a thank you wreath, call it Unity, a tribute to a new country, a new world.

Thanksgiving

Awaking to an avalanche of red and yellow maple leaves on the back porch. Squirrels and bunnies bathe in dancing November rain. A wreath on the door shines in the glory of orange hues. My child, adorned in a fall themed ruffle dress and hand-crafted velvet Mary Janes, picks a leaf, tearing it to shreds. She hugs my feet, looks into my eyes, as I stir creamy roasted pumpkin soup. Then pulls a hanging strand of wool from my flannel shirt, spinning it around her finger, a story to tell, the characters us, sitting at the table. A resplendent runner binds us in shimmer, Celtic tunes enrapture us. We pray in unison, devour corn, green beans, roasted potatoes, and diced turkey bound between slices of sourdough bread, simmering soup in a pot, brimming our thoughts. Pumpkin bread with vanilla pudding softens in our mouths. Oh, the sweetness of tomorrow's dreams.

Barbara Truncellito

Barbara Truncellito has published four collections of poetry, *In Fragile Twilight, Beyond the Seventh Poinsettia, Moonflowers,* and *In Tribes of Running Rain*. She holds a BA in English and an MS in management. She resides on Long Beach Island, NJ.

The Color Red

(in loving memory of my mother)

A rainbow dances
along walls of my house
where you lived
a sun-catcher its vessel
you in the color red
how it glowed
against your olive skin

As a child I remember asking
why are we washing and ironing
used clothes
giving it all to strangers
you replied because they are poor
once someone washed and ironed
a dress for me
it was red

Heart Beats

Light lingers
I hear you telling me
look into this band of colors
dance in its red
and give it away

A Winter Day

Palette of midday
pomegranates last scent
remnants of velvet
icicles dripping slowly
crash on the porch
recalling our days
simple in summer
sips of Chardonnay
circles of Venus
roses climbing through mist

My voice whispers
let me stroke your cheek
geraniums speak
of fuchsia and red
wind chimes sing
my bed is warm
I hear the wind
is it your voice

Day Lilies

Orange blossoms among seaweed
ask me to sing their song
through wind chimes
we dance for seven summers
citrus colors among languorous weeds
gently bend to sea breezes in august heat
lilies rest in twilight hues
tempt the sky with gentle kisses
sing our love song
as cardinals perch for a look
as the yellow moon nods

Bartholomew Barker

Bartholomew Barker is one of the organizers of Living Poetry, a collection of poets and poetry readers in the Triangle region of North Carolina. His first poetry collection, *Wednesday Night Regular*, written in and about strip clubs, was published in 2013. His second, *Milkshakes and Chilidogs*, a chapbook of food inspired poetry was served in 2017.

Born and raised in Ohio, studied in Chicago, he worked in Connecticut for nearly twenty years before moving to Hillsborough where he makes money as a computer programmer to fund his poetry habit.
Website: bartbarkerpoet.com

Limitless

I know the science

Some billions of years ago
the universe erupted into being
and some billions of years from now
the Sun will explode in a minor nova
and many trillions of years later
all the stars will go dark

But lying on this blanket
in some unsuspecting farmer's field
watching Perseid meteors
flare across the August sky
it all seems so
limitless

When I hold your hand

Sonnet for a Comet

With wandering Zeus and Ares
guarding my back, I hunt—
binoculars scanning distant
trees for something even further.

Orion won't help, he's resting
after a busy winter— this prey
is elusive and won't to return,
for a lifetime of lifetimes.

But the glow of the sun
just below the horizon
and the haze of humid summer
conspire to shield my quarry.

I won't have many more chances
but I'll try again tomorrow.

Summer Picnic

Fresh cut grass under our blanket
your warm skin 'neath my fingertips
a tree is blooming above us
and its petals envy your lips

The low branches waltz in the breeze
to the music guiding your hips
flowers open to catch the sun
and their petals envy your lips

That summer picnic long ago
like that bottle of wine we sipped
still I remember that blossom
how its petals envied your lips

Brian L. Hayes

Brian L. Hayes, Geologist, Poet, Cook, and Punster, lives in Piedmont North Carolina. While his career has been in environmental consulting, he prefers to cook and write. Hayes has published *Melancholy Love*, a chapbook. He is in three anthologies from India, including *Dreamers Never Die*. All are available on Amazon.

Pixie Goth

For Irum Iqbal

Sitting in the road
waiting for life
to come rolling by,
a great eighteen-wheeler
full of surprises
waiting to be unwrapped,
presents on Christmas morning,
a never-ending birthday.

a pretty pixie goth,
waiting for the music
to come rolling down
the labyrinth of alleyways,
sirens of the night,
calling your kindred spirits
to that eternal dance.

Still, you wait for a lover
to come and sweep you up,
fill all the holes,
aching in your heart.

Heart Beats

The Beloved is already
there within you,
eternal candle burning
to illuminate your heart.

©® 2020 Brian L Hayes
10/30/2020

Tropic Love

Dreams of a distant love
and the languid tropic days,
tall cold gin and tonics,
as the air shimmers in gentle waves.

Love was never torrid,
the nights were hot enough,
a measured, patient, passion,
courtship with a gentle touch.

Few words were ever spoken,
so much conveyed in a glance,
a brush of her fingertips
round and round in a subtle dance.

Words were never plain spoken,
everything in its own code,
lest prying ears nearby lurking,
discover a love was being sowed.

Heart Beats

Now in this land of winter,
As the snow is drifting high,
I long to see your smile,
and your brow arch above your eye.

©® 2020 Brian L Hayes
11/1/2020

Jewel of the Night

I came seeking the Beloved,
the precious jewel of the night,
with her long raven dark hair,
framing her round hempen face,
eyes that radiant polished jet.

I wait with my wine cup
Under the roof we first met,
An old man who seeks love,
Though heartbroken I've lost count,
hoping this time, it's real love for once.

Patently sitting through each night,
waiting the chariot of the new dawn,
chasing the darkness with its light,
banishing it to the shadow realm,
showing us the pathway home.

Heart Beats

O, Sweet Lady Sophia,
with a soft siren's song,
as I follow my path to the Beloved,
Saki stands waiting in the wineshop door,
To pour us a cup of the heady, dark, wine.

©® 2020 Brian L Hayes

10/8/2020

Bruce McRae

Bruce McRae, a Canadian musician currently residing on Salt Spring Island BC, is a multiple Pushcart nominee with over 1,600 poems published internationally in magazines such as *Poetry, Rattle*, and the *North American Review*. His books are *The So-Called Sonnets*, Silenced Press; *An Unbecoming Fit of Frenzy*, Cawing Crow Press; *Like as If*, Pski's Porch; *Hearsay,* The Poet's Haven.

A World Away

Another night scratching my head
as I reach for a pencil.
Another night spent torturing words
in the mind's muddied trenches,
proving that yes you can press money from guile
and oil from stone –
If you'd just continue squeezing please . . .
I'm reminded of other nights,
other battered moons and throw-away stars,
other dusky planets,
the alien writer there also
looking for the right words in the proper order;
holding the equivalent of a pencil
in what passes for a hand.

Carrie Levine

China born Australian Poet Jia-Li Yang (Cassa Bassa) works with the disadvantaged people in the community which gives her a special insight into those that suffer. She is constantly inspired by their resilience and strength.

An inquisitive writer that was a bit of a misfit as a child, she has blossomed into her writing.

Jia-Li's poetry has been published in the *Australian Poetry Journal Volume 8*, and *The Poets Symphony* published by Raw Earth Ink.

You may read more about her work on: flickerofthoughts.com

Heart Beats

Her Last Heart Beat

I saw grandma lying in the palliative unit
She was the last plum hanging on the branch
Although she survived the summer sun
Her overly ripen skin was purple and blue

We gathered around her like a flock of sheep
We retold the funny family stories
turning our tears into laughter
We kissed her clammy forehead and cool hands
We told her we loved her
and promised to see her in heaven
Her last heartbeat gave in
while the newborn birds chirping outside the window to welcome the golden sun

Greensleeves

The ocean looks extra boisterous in the middle of a heatwave

A sea of vibrant tents, umbrellas and cabanas scattering along the long stretch of beach line

Children are screeching in the cascades of white foams

Everything is intensifying the scorching sand beneath our feet

I pray silently for a break of cool breeze

The sound of Greensleeves is approaching like happy footsteps

I pause instantly and join in with others swarming towards the ice cream van

A new found joy springs up with the anticipation of cool relief

The familiar melody reminds me of the forever happy place

Ceinwen E Cariad Haydon

Ceinwen E Cariad Haydon lives near Newcastle upon Tyne, UK and writes short stories and poetry. She is widely published in online magazines and in print anthologies. Her first chapbook was published in July 2019: *Little Poems*, Hedgehog Press. Her first pamphlet is due to be published in 2021. She is a Pushcart Prize (2019 & 2020) and Forward Prize (2019) nominee and holds an MA in Creative Writing from Newcastle University, UK (2017). She believes everyone's voice counts.

acolyte

floss mists rise hang in morning's valley

dawn crowns rubbled escarpments
with potent peace

a winging curlew's cry shrills out
tastes bitter-sweet
stings like Kali's fresh slaps

Kali my goddess
free to dervish-dance
in her wild-handed circled heaven

she seduces tempts me to plunge

I surrender missed heartbeats

to swim in lakes of chaos

Heart Beats

I hold my breath
dive deep

bubbled moments surge

I surface gasp

my vital blood

scarlet as rosehips and rowan berries
on blasted storm-fast trees
quickens into life
debunks death rots apathy
into action spurs protection
and love for all our disparate peoples

Love's Shopping List

One pint of fresh milk of human kindness, drink deep

Live yeast proves love, raises crusty bread and spirits high

Ripe fruit sweetens daily life, fructose teases tastebuds alive

Spices relish long-houred days and later ginger chillied nights

Olive oil dresses salads or maybe emulsifies smooth mayonnaise

Balsamic tarts up lambs' lettuce leaves or acidifies crispy pommes frites

Tapas glorify finger foods shared, small portions sucked with relish and care

Rich cakes bake in preheated ovens, they satisfy hunger, carefully iced with flair

Cheese scones are good for al fresco picnics, slathered with butter or sour cream plumes

This list is a start, but don't assume or forget to explore your lovers' markets. Add your own treats

according to preference. For gastronomic adventures, search in the hidden niches of love's grand bazaar

Chanah Wizenberg

Chanah Wizenberg received her BA from Hunter College in English and Creative Writing. Her poetry has appeared in *TAF Stays Home, Poder, and Returning Woman's Magazine.* Chanah has been a professional ballerina, a pastry chef, and a High School English teacher. She resides in Raleigh, North Carolina with dog, Asha, and her cat, Marmalade.

The Fool

There you stand
at the edge of the cliff.
One more step and--
Let's not go there.

Instead let's look up
like you do
at the lemon looking sky.
Your little white pup at your heel.
He's hopping up on his hind quarters
looking at you.
Trying to get your attention?
Or equally happy looking at the sky.
It is wonderous to feel the warm gentle kiss
of the morning sun.
Welcoming the new day with joy
and play, with snow-capped mountain peaks
Just yonder there.

Heart Beats

You carry your traveler's stick
over your shoulder
at its end
your magic bag
carries all you need.

In your left hand
You hold a white rose
for pure intentions,
for innocence,
for new beginnings,
and the wisdom
you possess.

Because you know
the importance of
the leap of faith,
the universe,
the beginner's mind.

Heart Beats

Brushing Myself into a New Day

Brushing myself into a new day.
I rise with cadmium yellow,
light hue, then opera pink
with broad strokes of new gamboge,
and phthalo yellow green.

Painting gentle strokes for baby buds,
viridian vines for climbing trees, and crossing fields
with flowers to be, and roses red, and hear the
honeybees are humming, buzzing flower to flower.
The lavender and bluebells being delicate treats.

Upon return, the bees are
waggling and dancing their figure 8's
alerting workers to the best sweets.

Robins perching high above
singing love songs
while woodpeckers are drumming,
squirrels are exploring, while
the tree sap is flowing, and
the earth's rich perfume is permeating the air.

Heart Beats

Then the peeper's sing their songs
while I'm painting soft strokes
of gentle sea blues,
and lavender hues,
with transparent yellows,
and perinone orange.
I slide behind the mountain
a cardamom red.

Finding Home

It was weeks before the silence
became comfortable

In the beginning
it was hell
there were nightmares and panic attacks
flashbacks and setbacks

Had to snap myself back
into the present
again, again, and again

Why am I torturing myself?

Running
I've been running
away from myself
afraid

Heart Beats

Time

to stop made to stop
by the Pandemic
because we must Stay-at-Home
safe-at-Home
Safe-at-Home
safe

Time

To sit still and dig deep
within myself *my* self

Time

To ask, what is it *you* want?
just you
not *them*

Heart Beats

Time

Stop
Looking for acceptance
for approval

Time

To start looking inside
so, I turned off the tv
opened the balcony door
and sat in my easy chair and
listened

In the beginning
the silence screamed at me
but then, I heard the birds sing
and a crow came to visit me
perching on the balcony
cawing at me
while genuflecting
his intention to me
before flying away from me
returning to me
the next day

Heart Beats

and the next
for a week

What did it all mean?
A relative calling me?

And then I heard her voice calling me
From beyond, Nonnie called
And so, I
listened
that's when she spoke to me
loving me
telling me
to be
panic free, nightmare free
and   *you* are free
you *are* home

Chyrel J. Jackson

Chyrel J. Jackson is an avid lover, reader, and writer of African American Literature. She grew up in a Southern Suburb of Chicago, IL. Influenced by the Literary works of James Baldwin, Toni Morrison, Maya Angelou, Langston Hughes, Nikki Giovanni, and Sonia Sanchez, Jackson writes in the Spirit of these ancestors. Giving a voice to social issues that plague our modern time.

Along with her sister, Lyris D. Wallace, they published *Different Sides of the Same Coin*, a modern collage of poetry as experienced from the Black female perspective of 2 sisters and authors. This work is an interesting twist on Harlem Renaissance revisited as it collides with 2020 social struggles of our current time.

Poetry, Political Opinion editorials, Book reviews and have an unpublished children's book. Poetry is Jackson's preferred genre of choice. You can find her on Sistersrocnrhyme.com

Love Unspoken

An elongated stare.
The small circle
of your arms with
just enough space
only for me.
A gentle caress upon
my cheek.
The soothing tug
of my hand.
One tender and ever
so slight forehead
kiss lets me
know of your need
to feel
closer to me.
I, too, am longing
for your heat.
Is it possible we
have developed our
very own presumed
unstated dialog?

Heart Beats

I look in your eyes
and they greet me
with that almost secret
as if hidden only for
me to see smile.
We have mastered our
personally distinct
unspoken language
of love.

    cjj '20

Morning Ritual

Every day two very
familiar lovers part
ways for a time...
As Mr. leaves HER
at bedside while HE
prepares himself
for HIS daily grind.

    WORK...
HE lovingly,
    knowingly,
gazes at HER sleeping
form as SHE lays
soundly asleep in
HIS bed.
    Sleeping...

HE lovingly,
   knowingly,
admires HER.
HIS eyes convey
ALL mere words
could ever repetitively
say...
Lovingly,
   knowingly,
"Damn, I love that
woman".

    cjj '20

Warring Members

My arms
  long to embrace
      you
My hands
   wish to be held
      by yours
My eyes
   want to behold you
      forever,
today, tomorrow; for always,
     my love.
My lips
   long to kiss
      you

Heart Beats

My ears
    wish to hear
        you speak
because of you, my
    heart and mind
        remain in mortal war
today, tomorrow, for always,
        my love.

        cjj'98

Colin James

Colin James has a couple of chapbooks of poetry published. *Dreams of The Really Annoying* from Writing Knights Press and *A Thoroughness Not Deprived of Absurdity* from Piski's Porch Press and a book of poems, *Resisting Probability*, from Sagging Meniscus Press

Amelia Earhart's Arrival

Those hiphuggers really suit you
They are hiphuggers aren't they?
Just the standard pilot pants.
Flexible vertical ridges brusque before
the acquiescence of Jet Magazine.
Monsters regaled in National Geographic.
Beauty is a flamboyant word
I never use it.
Those eyes staring back
attributable to any
clever sleight of hand.

Pedantic Pleasures and the Nonessential

The White Mountains
and The Brown Mountains
fought o'er the green valley.
My credit card was useless
else I would have bought the road,
just a dirt track really
connecting or separating.
Moss nowhere to be seen.
My bank manager absolutely refuses
to take my calls.
Oblivious to the can't miss,
chairman of the two-foot putt.
A golf course then or something
just as environmentally inconvenient.
The sun had yet to reveal its bias.

Danielle Martin

As a Caribbean woman and mother, Danielle Martin crafts poetry with a distinct vibe and intensity innate of her experiences and culture. However, she believes we are all versions of each other. Meeting at different stages or sometimes barely touching as we slide through life's chaotic dimensions. Writing is her solace and *Kissing Shadows: Caribbean Love Poems* was her first published Anthology of poetry.

Additionally, her work has been featured in several publications, *Ariel Chart, Claudius Speaks, Free Lit Magazine, the 2016 and 2017 Poetry Marathon Anthologies* and most recently the *Organic Poet*.

Danielle currently spends her time engaged in writing workshops and drinking copious amounts of coffee.

Her favorite mantra is... "And this too shall pass."

Happiness… it's never where you think you'll find it.

Waves whipping against darkened shorelines
fishes
escaping
death with tugs and jerks
playing
with fishermen's pockets

Salty winds driving bones to shiver
iridescent
laughter
like an old steel-pan
melody
under a laden moon

Mottled shades of undulating greens
beckoning
fertility
from afar

raindrops

evaporating upon silky cocoa pod skin

And lessons unravelling in our yearnings for

freedom

Battimamzelles

they zig-zag before the storm

wings

the last flicker from departed souls

Forcing one to stop as

grandma's

beautiful

words whisper like

yesterday

"You'll always know when I'm near."

Dorothy La Motta

Dorothy La Motta is a children's book author, poet, and published freelance writer.

She focuses mainly on juvenile fiction, non-fiction, and poetry. She serves on the 'Critique' team of the Johnson County Writers Group. Dorothy resides in North Carolina.

Dreamy Nights

It all started with a dreamy night under a moonlit sky and twinkling stars above.

Two lovers met and romance bloomed. And from that dreamy night, my tiny self was born. Mom's happy tears fell upon my fine blond curly hair. I felt her cradle my soft, pink, naked body to her breast as love formed an unbroken bond.

Years passed all too quickly. I grew up much too fast. I met my first love Vinnie on a beachfront dreamy night. We walked barefoot in the creamy sand, tenderly holding hands. The salty waves rolled in caressing the shore and leaving its misty spray on our cheeks.

It didn't take long to know our hearts were beginning to dance. Our parted lips met, as our eyes locked in a silent gaze, enchanted by our tender kiss. Our youth still unsure of what was happening with the strange sensations our bodies felt.

The clock ticked forward at accelerated speed encapsulating our hearts together. We were falling in love. On a warm, dreamy night, as nightingales sang their evening symphony, Vinnie proposed under the boughs of a mighty oak, just as the moon made its glowing, grand entrance, and the sun gracefully bidding adieu below the horizon. We were alone in

a moment of magical bliss nestled in each other's sweet embrace.

As love grew, plans were made, vows were kept, dreams came true, and prayers were answered. And, on one star-studded, dreamy night that lit up the sky like diamonds scattered on a jeweler's velvet cloth, our baby daughter, Maria Antoinette was born.

My happy tears fell upon her fine blond curly hair as I cradled her soft, pink, naked body to my breast as love formed an unbroken bond.

And it all started with one dreamy night-

The Business Trip

For just a little while my love, I must leave you once again
When I take you in my arms, I feel the beating of your heart
I wipe your tears so sad and weave your soft hands in mine
A hug, a kiss, a warm caress, my treasure when we're apart

I'm packed and ready, but my feet don't want to move
The gas tank is filled, but silent my car waits
My GPS at my command is ready to impress
My smartphone is charged to help me not be late

The front door still closed; the lock not yet opened
When I step outside, I'm leaving the love of my life behind
Your lavender perfume lingers permeating my very being
You're a flower with open petals, sending a scented whiff sublime
It doesn't matter where I stay, you're always on my mind
And as the diamond studded stars float across the azure sky,
They'll twinkle a wink or two as I wave my shaking hand
My tear-drenched eyes, a fleeting glance, a weakened sad goodbye

Heart Beats

Just wait a while longer dear and soon the days will pass,

When God will guide me home again to wipe your happy tears

It's then I'll long for you to whisper sweet nothings in my ear

As you curl your arms around me and tell me words, I want to hear

Get ready to dance and laugh again at the end of my business trip

When our two lips meet again, and our hearts will beat as one

A love like ours is very rare as priceless diamonds are

For true love cannot be silenced it's a song that must be sung

Elizabeth O. Ogunmodede

Elizabeth O. Ogunmodede is a Nigerian teen author who is a co-author of two poetry books and an author of two other books on Amazon. She is the oldest of three kids and she lives with her parents in Nigeria. She presently attends high school in Nigeria, and she is currently working on a poetry-based novel with her mentor, Jill Sharon Kimmelman while working on a book of her own.

Heart Beats

The Beauty of Togetherness

I sat with my brethren around the bonfire,
Playing the game of would you rather?
under the blanket of the sky,
with shining stars to light up the night,
I snuggled under my blanket,
whispering into the night with my friend,
her voice, a soothing balm and a salve,
Could anything be more beautiful,
than confiding in a trustworthy friend?
Could the Easter or the Thanksgiving,
or the Yule be celebrated,
without the smile of a loved one?
If you know the beauty of togetherness,
then I believe, you'd understand the beauty,
of faces, lit up by smiles around you

Heart Beats

My Heart Leaped

Poetry is the twin of magic,
one like you would understand its power
Poetry is a language that can be understood,
by the inhabitants of its land,
I know you can tell,
Poetry makes you travel through,
the beauty of a powerful picture,
that strong image that's painted in your mind
And poetry fits you into a story
I believe you know
It all seems like yesterday fella,
When I wrote my first poem,
When I wrote my own first language,
When I began to build my world,
And I remember--- that my heart leaped for joy

Frank Hubeny

Frank Hubeny spends his time between Miami Beach, FL, and Northbrook, IL. He has appeared in Snakeskin and The Lyric. He regularly posts poems, prose, and photography at frankhubeny.blog.

Grow

I wasn't there to plant this spring.
The morning glories didn't care.
They're back again off climbing where
I left some soil. No watering
but they still rose. It's comforting
that when I fail, they ever grow
although forgotten. Watch them show
their bright green leaves each like a heart.
I see the buds break out and start
to bloom again. There! Off they go.

Worn

Many people, up and down,
have worn the stone treads thin.
The weeds have taken root in cracks.
And I? I fit right in.

Ivor Steven

Ivor was formerly an Industrial Chemist, then a Plumber, and now retired, and he lives in Geelong, Australia He has had numerous poems published, in on-line magazines such as, *Spillwords, Vita Brevis*, and *Free Verse Revolution*. He has also been represented in many anthology publications. He is the Author of the poetry book "*Tullawalla*".

Recently he was appointed to the "*Go Dog Go Café*" magazine's website team of Baristas. He is also an active member of the Geelong Writers Inc. and many of his poems are published in their annual Anthologies.

Clear Blue Jar

Laying here looking above
Staring toward the sky
Wondering why
Why is our sky blue?
How do we perceive hues?
And why say "Feeling blue"
When it is not true
The blue I see
Is no-one's fool
So why fool with me
Seeing every new face
Has your forever smile
Yours on every dial
Like yesterday's last mile
Doing your time in style
Smiling faces, new and old alike
Beaming, even from afar
Smiling at my new life
My life in a clear blue jar

Downhill Run

I was dreaming

Plotting and scheming

I followed you skiing

Running the slopes gliding

Twists and twirls

Loops and hoops

Downhill and dancing

Our hearts were racing

Spirals and swirls

Joyous smiles

Swishing faster and faster

Swooping last to first

Silver and gold

Winners and grinners

Your curls unfurl

Ruby hair unfolds

Beauty I behold

Frozen bliss

We kiss

Soul to soul

A Festival

A Festival, beside the sea
Musicians playing in the breeze
Song-catchers of sadness and glee
Open for everyone to see

A Festival, of warmth and love
Bound together within a community glove
Endless tunes, over and above
Gliding around like peaceful doves

A Festival, with friends in a cottage
Laughter, travelling through the village
Riding on a horse-drawn carriage
Singing out of tune, a broken homage

A Festival, rejoicing day and night
Eating and drinking on-site
The multitude happy and bright
Hovering under the stage lights

Heart Beats

A Festival, a joyful blast
Memories always to last
The fun time went so fast
Holding hands on the grass

Jaya Avendel

Jaya Avendel is a word witch from the Blue Ridge Mountains of Virginia, writing family into fantasy through poetry and prose. Her writing is published at *Visual Verse, Free Verse Revolution,* and *Spillwords Press*, among others, as well as having appeared in *As the World Burns* from Indie Blu(e) Publishing. She writes at ninchronicles.com.

Listening

Cardinal in the apple tree
Vibrant red female
Oddity.

Osprey against the blue sky
Cloudy underbelly
Hungry.

Secrets from the house next door
Alive in the wind
Curious.

Lone teapot glazed earthen
Row of chipped cups
Perfect.

Assurances

Roses in the ashes are
Preferable to flowers in
Painted vases.
Dead petals have lived proudly while
Life is still learning to embrace fire.

Community

In song I wrap myself
The troubles of the world dim.

I dance
For the single snowflake struggling against the sun
For the lone crow on a flagpole
For the roses flowering in December.
Some people look away
Seeking to spare me embarrassment.

Others join in and dance
For the oddly shaped cups that make tea sweeter
For the knife that grandmother held
For expression.

Here are the souls who turn the earth and make it golden
Here are the souls who stop me counting the days on the calendar
Here are the souls who make my heart sing.

I need no other music.

JeanMarie Olivieri

JeanMarie Olivieri is a mostly retired business writer who keeps trying to become a short story writer, but it keeps coming out as poetry. She has been published in online journals and anthologies. She is a co-organizer for the Living Poetry Meetup group, and an editor for the Heron Clan Poetry Anthology series. Follow her at jeanmarieolivieri.wordpress.com/

Holey Satisfied

I got holes in my shoes.
They've got ventilation.
But don't you worry.
I'll make my destination.

I got holes in my jeans,
my knees poke through.
But you won't see my undies
cause my seat seam is true.

I got a hole in my wallet,
all my money is gone.
I can't buy anything
cause I'm overdrawn.

Don't worry about my holey ventilation.
It helps with the heat and the perspiration.

Coffee

The cat meows me into the kitchen
every morning for my Daily Medication
of bean and sugar and cream.

A midafternoon slump calls
for Columbian Roast
and the illusion of industry.

Living is better with the chemical elixir
of hot brewed go-go juice,
400 million cups a day in America.

The bitter flavor of the daily grind
sweetened into candy drops or ice-cream
satisfies, but doesn't say
> Sit with me,
> I've got news,
> or, I like you

like a cup of joe

Jill Sharon Kimmelman

Jill Sharon Kimmelman was nominated for a Pushcart Prize, in Poetry and Best of The Net 2018. Publications include *Vita Brevis Press, Spillwords Press, Yasou! A Celebration of Life Ezine, Compositor, Writing in A Woman's Voice blogspot, Poetic Musings, Delaware Boots on The Ground,* and *Better Than Starbucks.*

Her passions include reading aloud, cooking from the heart, theatre, lively book discussions, and photography. She lives in Delaware with her husband Tim and is the proud mother of her son Jordan.

The Water Bearer

A mythic thunderbolt crashed inside of me

zero hour nine a:m

settling somewhere between my head and my heart

It is kicking at my chest...a savage with hunger pains...

knocking with an insistent relentlessness...yet oddly welcome

You release my passions as I release my poems

pouring out like cool clear water from an ancient copper jug

So when you call out to me...I will answer you

in the voice of the water bearer

@Jill Sharon Kimmelman, Autumn 2020

In Six Days

(for Katrina and Adam)

In six days
pristine snow will fall again
the air will be filled with the scent of newly arrived-winter
frilling the ground...creating lacy patterns with our shoes

In six days
we will share warm-made-from-scratch-cocoa
discover a delight in devouring whispery confections of
buttery toffees and chocolate truffles

In six days
we will crawl beneath our wedding ring quilt...holding hands to catch each other's dreams
the tangle of our limbs...a perfect jigsaw puzzle

Morning dawns...and in six more days
we will join together...at last...perfectly remade

@Jill Sharon Kimmelman, Autumn 2019

A Single Decision

If you found them at your door
a crush of summer's vibrant blossoms
alluring...breathtaking...compelling
dropped without so much as a note
near-to-wilting...from hours without water
would you take them in or toss them out?

They will still bloom beautifully
releasing their potent nectar in sweet-dashes-of-scent
because they were rescued...just in time...by you

@Jill Sharon Kimmelman Spring 2020

Joan McNerney

Joan McNerney's poetry is found in many literary magazines such as *Seven Circle Press, Dinner with the Muse, Poet Warriors, Blueline,* and *Halcyon Days*. Four *Bright Hills Press Anthologies*, several *Poppy Road Journals*, and numerous *Poets' Espresso Reviews* have accepted her work. She has four Best of the Net nominations. Her latest title is *The Muse in Miniature* available on Amazon.com and Cyberwit.net

Winter Solstice

Hurry, short days are here,
too much to do.
Get ready, find gloves,
hats, scarves, sweaters.

Stopping to see the
shape of a snowflake.
Coming home to luxuriate
in dim light listening

to heat hissing and finding
warmth from hot teas.
Bundled in bed comforted by
mounds of blankets, books.

Finally succumbing to
our northern goddess,
whose black nights are long
and silent as evergreens.

Heart Beats

Winter Watch

Tangled…one ragged
leaf clings to the bough.

Winter storm warning…
headlights beam at noon.

Frost pinches my cheeks
my cool cruel lover.

Came home just in time
for the first dizzy dance
of December flurries.

More amazing than
redwood forests…
your ice blue eyes.

Heart Beats

Simmering soup fills my
kitchen with aromas.

 All day my windows
chatter like nervous teeth.

Crystals spin together in
joyful pirouette…a cool ballet.

Wintry Bouquet

This December
during wide nights
hemmed by blackness,
I remember roses.
Pink, yellow, red violet
those satin blooms of June.

We must wait six months
before seeing blossoms,
touch their brightness
crush their scent
with fingertips.

Now there are only
ebony pools of winter's
heavy ink of darkness.

Heart Beats

Dipping into memory of
my lips touching petals
tantalizing sweet buds.
My body longs for softness.

I glimpse brilliant faces of
flowers right before me as I
burrow beneath frosty blankets.
Bracing against that long, cold
nocturnal of wind and shadow.

John Lambremont, Sr.

John Lambremont, Sr. is from Baton Rouge, Louisiana. John's poems have been published in many journals, including *Pacific Review, The Louisiana Review,* and *The Minetta Review*. John's collections include two published in 2018: *Old Blues, New Blues*, by Pski's Porch Publishing, and *The Book of Acrostics*, by Truth Serum Press.

A Child of Many Villages

Threads of life will weave,
once given the chance,
a beautiful mixed flower
of distinction and refinement.

Kaine is our rainbow baby,
an angel here on earth,
and everyone's delight.
His threads are black, yellow, and white.
His blood is African, Vietnamese,
French, German, Belgian, and
Welsh, with a bit of Chinese thrown in,
but he is and always will be
an American.

His eyes are blue at times,
other times they are green.
His hair is curly and black,
and his skin olive.
He is smothered with love,
and everyone wants to hold him.

Let me show you pictures of my grandson.

Loukia (an acrostic)

Little one, you came to us so tender and so meek;
Only now you're showing us that you have got some cheek;
Underneath the mobile you have uttered cries of joy,
Kicking your legs up and down and staring at your toys;
In time, you will run to us and jump into our arms;
Always we will give you love and allay all your qualms.

A Big Birthday for Nhu-Y (an acrostic)

Honey-toned is your skin, and Honey my name for you;
Always has been this way, and it always has been true;
Understanding and caring among your great virtues.

Today is a special day; though you say it's not so;
Happiness I bring to you, and happiness you show;
In the end, a better friend I know I'll never know.

Never have I loved you more, and rest this day assured
Heaven is on earth with you; your thoughts, your acts, your words;
Until we are parted, I will always love you so;
Yet, forever we will be together as love grows.

José Rafael Castilleja

José Rafael Castilleja is a writer, poet, and community leader.

Heart Beats

Calming the Storm

In the patio,
In the South,
From March till now
My Heart beats slow,
Back to normal
With all my parents
Feline cats.

Yin-Yang is her favorite cat.
Her lit green tinted eyes
Slender white nose.

In her eyes you can see
The mother, the crafty thoughts,
The love and kindness.

Garfield is cat king.
His favorite cat, we believe.
A much older cat.
Yet muscular and ladies cat.
In his eyes you can see
The hunter, the strong will,

Heart Beats

The strength and discipline.

Tranquil and calm comes over,
The world becomes smaller,
My breathe is calmer.
Another day.

We believe
Unity is near.

Spanish Translation of Calming the Storm

Calmando la Tormenta

En una plaza
En el sur
Desde marzo hasta ahora
Mi corazón lentamente canta
Volver a la normalidad
Con todos los gatos felinos
De mis padres.

Ying-Yang es su gato favorito.
Sus ojos teñidos de verde encendido
Nariz blanca y delgada.

En sus ojos puedes ver
La madre, el astuto pensamiento
El amor y la bondad.

Garfield es el rey gato

Su gato favorito, creemos.

Sus ojos teñidos de azul claro

Un gato mucho mayor

Sin embargo, gato musvuloso

Y Casanova con las damas.

En sus ojos puedes ver

El cazador, el fuerte voluntad

La fuerza y la disciplina.

Tranquila y calma viene

El mundo se vuelve más pequeño

Mi respiración es más tranquila

Otro dia.

Nosotros creemos

La unidad está cerca.

Beautiful in red

Who is she?
She makes my heart beat.
I was older than her in the 90s
Yet the years did not matter.

I went on several date with her.
She was nice, sweet, and beautiful.

We went all over town.
To the ice cream shop,
To the drive-in fast food,
To the movies,
And even to the short shot golf.

You and I were meant to be together.

Yet it did not last.
I grow up,
Got a job upstate.

We will always have
Our time together.

Best wishes to your
New owner of my

Old 1989 mustang.

Joyce Lindenmuth

Joyce Lindenmuth has been writing since her teen years but has taken poetry writing seriously since she joined a writing group in 2014. Since then, Joyce has been published in chapbooks and anthologies. Her love of nature is her primary stimulus for her poetry. She is a retired hospice social worker and lives on beautiful Lake Gaston in Virginia.

Escape

I recline comfortably in a chair on my lakeside deck
quiet afternoon respite
from the shoulds waiting in the house behind me

soft breezes slide over my skin and tousle my hair
gentling the heavy heat of the summer day

far below small waves lap lazily against the shore
reaching the end of a journey started somewhere far away
soothing sound like the heartbeat of the earth

wispy clouds drift languidly across the milky blue
panorama of the sky
not bothering to sculpt images, content with gauzy tatters

late day sunshine casts silver coins of light upon the water
laid upon the ruffled surface of the wavelets
glittering far as the eye can see

across the lake, trees lining the roller-coaster shoreline
resplendent in their summer green soothe my spirit

only occasional boat noise disturbs the quiet
I breathe out slowly, letting the interruption slide away
inner turmoil quieted

for now

Evening Walk

air crisp and cool
each in-drawn breath refreshing my soul
sweet whiffs of honeysuckle
soothe my senses

leaves and branches
softly droop
as if exhausted from
their long day fighting winds
and reaching for
life-giving rays of sunshine

the bird choir
blending voices since dawn
diminishes to an occasional
solo chirp
finally stilling

squirrels make leaf-rustling noises
as they scamper to nests
high in the canopy
cricket and frog songs signal
encroaching night

a coppery sun slides
slowly into the horizon
offering little competition
to the eager moon
as it slices insistently through
a still brilliant blue envelope of sky

random cloud whisps
drift upward
dissipate into the moon
a hush pervades the twilight
evening walk over
peace reigns

Winter Gift

snow fell in a torrent of fat flakes
like feathers ripped from the down pillow of clouds
fragments landing softly
noiselessly
absorbed by the warm earth of yesterday
still the feathers fell
undaunted
determined
steady
flake by flake
white began to clothe the drab shapes of sleeping winter
night fell
darkness masking the silent settling of snow

morning brought sunshine
the dome of sky solid azure blue
clouds having yielded their mass to the earth
yesterday's branches
so barren
so plain
shine

as if all the stars hidden by the night's clouds
fell one by one, embracing each branch
in spectacular brilliance

cold air defied the sun's valiant rays
refusing to melt the sparkling snow
days of unusual winter warmth overcome
in a brief wondrous surprise visit
staying just long enough
just a day
a reminder that winter has gifts to give

Karla Linn Merrifield

Karla Linn Merrifield has had 800+ poems appear in dozens of journals and anthologies. She has 14 books to her credit. Following her 2018 *Psyche's Scroll* (Poetry Box Select) is the 2019 full-length book *Athabaskan Fractal: Poems of the Far North* from Cirque Press. She is currently at work on a poetry collection, *My Body the Guitar*, inspired by famous guitarists and their guitars; the book is slated to be published in December 2021 by Before Your Quiet Eyes Publications Holograph Series (Rochester, NY). Tweet @LinnMerrifiel

Heart Beats

Swamp Psalm of the Water Sprite

The Fakahatchee is my shepherdess;

I shall not want for canopied swamps.

She maketh me to submerge below profligate

fronds and tendrils.

She leadeth me into still waters.

She restoreth my arid hope.

She leadeth me along slow flowing

strands of wildness for her faith sake.

Yea, though I wade through the valley

in the shadows of fishing spiders

beside alligator ponds, I fear not greed,

for thou, green queen, art with me, in me.

Thy sword ferns and ghost orchids

do comfort me.

Heart Beats

Thou preparest a cypress stand before me

in the cool space of my heart.

Thou annointest my soul with dew.

My dream runneth over in liquid light.

Surely chlorophyll and oxygen

shall follow me all the breaths of my life

and I shall dwell in thy habitat

of epiphyte, lichen, and moss—forever.

Safety Instructions

Cross Orleans County cornfields in March
in brimmed hat & mukluks;
geese above & mud below welcome spring.

Journey down Colorado River rapids in May
in a dory with trustworthy spouse;
greet so many dangers in paradise.

Dive into Lake Ontario this summer
with both eyes wide open;
salmon will seek your company.

In autumn climb Baxter Mountain's steep trail
with your best friend;
peak beauty can cause dizziness.

Return again to West Virginia coal mines collapsed
in '69, hear daddy's ghostly prayers;
cave-ins happen any time, everywhere.

Visit again also those graveyards at Hector,
arm in arm with two sisters, one brother;
our chanting may skein new nets of hope.

In winter, read this poem with both hands holding
open pages while seated comfortably at home;
words slay doubts great, small, staggering, passing.

Karol Nielsen

Karol Nielsen is the author of memoirs: *Black Elephants* (Bison Books, 2011) and *Walking A&P* (Mascot Books, 2018), chapbooks: *This Woman I Thought I'd Be* (Finishing Line Press, 2012) and *Vietnam Made Me Who I Am* (Finishing Line Press, 2020). Her first memoir was shortlisted for the William Saroyan International Prize for Writing in nonfiction in 2012. Her full poetry collection was a finalist for the Colorado Prize for Poetry in 2007. Her work has appeared in *Epiphany, Guernica, Lumina, North Dakota Quarterly, Permafrost, RiverSedge*, and elsewhere. She has taught writing at New York University and New York Writers Workshop.

Instagram

I joined Instagram to promote my upcoming book, but it soon became a place to share artistic images of mosaics, architectural details, mountains, spring flowers, and poems. I collected over 1,000 followers. Some congratulated me when my book came out, but hundreds endorsed my artistic photos, including a sketch from a time before writing took over as my way to express myself. I followed poets but quickly I was drawn to the minimalist subculture that turns cropped angles of buildings into art. I developed crushes on strangers and was devastated when a young hipster said he stopped posting a year ago after his accident. What accident? He didn't say. He posted selfies in a stack and when I flipped through, I saw his prosthetic leg. I didn't know what to say to this stranger who had suffered like this. I follow a woman who lost 300 pounds and underwent surgery to remove her loose skin. She is upbeat and inspiring even when haters trash her for gaining back some weight. I follow some celebrities, too, like the cast of a teen television series I binge watch over and over. It feels frivolous, a guilty pleasure like Boston Cream donuts. Then one of the actors from the show posted wise words from O. Henry: "Write what you like; there is no other rule."

Listener

Over dinner, she told us her ideas about the news and politics while we listened. She had been in my writer's group and we remained close even though the group no longer met. She stopped herself and said, I'm doing all the talking; neither of you has said a word. Her friend chimed in with a little something, but her soft-spoken voice was hard to hear in the noisy French bistro. We briefly discussed my essay that had been published in a literary magazine, but I couldn't sustain the momentum. She went back to talking about the news and politics and we were quiet. When I told my mother what happened, she said she stopped being embarrassed by her silence when she realized a family friend, she respected was silent, too. The world needs listeners, she said, and I listened to her.

Kathy Jo (Blake) Bryant

Kathy Jo (Blake) Bryant lives in California. She is a Domestic Engineer, an avid genealogist, and a member of a lineage society, authoring a two-volume book on genealogy. They have published her in *Bharath Vision, The Sparrow, Open Door Poetry Magazine* and she has received many certificates for her work. Her poems can be found on her Facebook page, "Poetree."

Heartbeat Happiness

What makes my heart
just beat with joy…
A butterfly with wings in flight?
A bird's song echoing with delight?

What makes your heart
just beat with joy…
A baby's coo as they see your face?
The cheering crowd as you win a race?

What makes their heart
Just beat with joy…
Their mother's test, now cancer free?
Their child securing a college degree?

What makes our hearts
Just beat with joy…
Sweet compliments a friend may say?
After a storm…. the sun's bright ray?

Whoever or wherever you are today...

May Heartbeat Happiness come your way!

"Poetree" © November 10, 2020

The Sound of the Harp

The sound of the harp,
   Brings a solace so calm.
It delights ready ear,
   And diffuses sweet balm.

A foretaste of Heaven,
   Harmonies so sublime.
They transcend our senses,
   As our ecstasies climb!

May our hearts be transformed,
   And our souls be renewed,
As we listen, entranced,
   To arpeggio and etude!

May each of our lives,
   Spread a joy so replete,
Like a well- tuned harp,
   Will bring happiness, complete!
"Poetree" © July 22, 2020

Majestic Mountains

Majestic Mountains speak to me…
   So grand a monument to power.
They rise with grandeur to the skies…
   Just like a strong and awesome tower…

The forest folk are dwellers there…
   Trees are like the mountain's hair.
As some are lush with verdant growth.
   Yet others are just bald and bare…

In Spring and Summer oft, you'll see…
   Bright flowers growing here and there.
They're such a wondrous sight to view.
   A crown to decorate her hair…

In Autumn she will dye her hair…
   With colors bright and colors fair…
This is a gorgeous sight to see…
   Just like a lovely rainbow there!

In Winter she will often wear…
   A cap of snow upon her hair…
So picturesque, and beautiful….
   Folks often want to ski up there...

The mountains call to you and me…
    "Come, one, come all…my trails to see."
Our voices echo through her jags…
    "We are right here, among your crags!"

"Poetree" © November 16, 2020

Katie Jenkins

Katie Jenkins lives in Gloucestershire, England, with her husband and son. Her poetry has been published online by various UK and international journals and anthologized by *Everyman's Library* and *Acid Bath Publishing*. She has a creative writing diploma with distinction from Oxford University.

Amongst all the potentialities of the universe

here is my son,
all knock knees and clavicle,
emerging from the pool.

Here too, is the shampoo
I placed in our un-secret
secret place

for him to find, faith
materialised, an everyday kind
of miracle.

Nocturne

the doppler swoosh of passing cars

headlight beams slicing dark

radio babble low over engine hum

warm blowers on

white lines flash alongside

but we are suspended in time

gone and not arrived

light passes over

the mirror's sleeping child

drooping head swaying in motion

his shapely mouth open

Heart Beats

cupid's bow loosing

puffs of angel breath

lash-lines like shy smiles

cheeks curved like the earth

rushing by underneath us

Marriage Review

I'm thinking of swapping you for another one,
it's been ten years since our wedding day,
and I fear that love, as love does, may have gone.

I've a few years left, I think, before I'm done,
I look like myself if I cover my grey.
Perhaps, while I can, I should try out another one.

Perhaps the apotheosis of our love was our son,
and he is a compelling reason to stay,
but not if love has gone.

I don't look like I did at twenty-one –
I wonder if you have ever thought to stray,
to see how it might be with another one.

Perhaps I've already been cheated on
and you haven't been brave enough to say.
Maybe your love for me has gone.

Sometimes, though, when we are alone,
you still look at me in your dream-eyed way.
No, I won't swap you for another one.
Love may have changed, but has not gone.

Krzystof "Christopher" T. Dabrowski

Krystof "Christopher" T. Dabrowski is a Polish writer and screenwriter. His books have been published in Poland, the USA, Spain and Germany. His stories were published in many countries: USA, England, Australia, Canada, Poland, Russia, Germany & India. And he published his stories in the following magazines: *PLAYBOY* (Slovak edition), USA, England, Czech Republic, Russia, Brasil, Spain, Argentina, Germany, Italy, Hungary, Mexico, Albania & Nigeria. He can be found on Facebook: Krzystof-T-Dabrowski, Amazon, and his Website.

The different

They thought I was a freak; I was sitting despite the bustle...

I was wrapped in velvet silence, so I kept sitting.

They thought I was a hobo. My hair had grown. I started to stink.

They thought I am deaf. They were screaming. I didn't react.

They mocked me. I didn't defend myself.

Instead of pupils, I had eye whites.

They thought I was a madman because didn't eat or drink.

They locked me in a laboratory. They examined, punctured, experimented without any results.

They couldn't understand what happened to me.

I was simply immersed in very deep meditation.

Translated by Julia Mraczny

Lauren M. Clemmons

Growing up in North Carolina, Lauren M. Clemmons spent many hours as a child writing stories and poems. Although the demands of her adult-work-life interrupted her creative writing, she has begun writing again and recently published an essay in an anthology. She aspires to create and publish more pieces.

Fancy Green Fronds

Those fancy dark green fronds stuck atop their pineapple-like lollipop sticks

    Wind-dancing, moving to the tune of the Ocean Air

    Looking like spiky tangles of bed head---

        Swinging to the left; swaying to the right; then a pause…

        Now! Going-WILD with Full Frond-head-SWIRLS

            As the Ocean Air hits its windy-Crescendo with impatience.

And then, I see Them. Through the window, down the walkway, over the sea-oats sand dunes, and on the shore of the flat-glass Ocean protecting the horizon---

    Summer Images.

She is running on the sand in the water's edge, lean strong legs,

Her bodyboard flopping carefree on its rope leash,

Heart Beats

Hitting the sandy shore left and right behind Her.

Like a gazelle, I think. She makes running look effortless. I smile.

She gives Him the board's leash and positions herself tummy-down, hands gripping the board's sides.

He is running now and pulling Her along the shoreline through inches high surf.

He is strong and determined and powerful. It's as if He carries himself on air.

He is so fast, and I am watching flawless movement.

He is laughing; He is free; but my mother's heart has been captured by love and pride.

She is skimming across the water's edge now on a magic Styrofoam carpet powered by Her Brother and bumping on sand swirls.

Then He whips the board full circle to the left, turning her in the opposite direction.

She grabs the board's edges tightly;

He is Running with Her, pulling her away from me, but they return again on the next loop.

Over and over They repeat this Game. If She falls off the board, She gets back on.

And there the Two go again----

My Boy and My Girl, on a summer's day

When the Sun and Ocean played with Them, and the Sand held Them near me;

Always close to my heart; a memory, a joy, easily within reach.

And those fancy green fronds keep dancing in the wind, pleasingly amusing, diverting me with their frolic,

Even now, as I walk through crisp fall leaves.

A Mother's Blessing to Her Daughter

Once upon a time,
    I said I love you.
Beautiful baby, Golden spirit
    The tiniest feet in my palm---will someday move you through life
    The tiniest hands that I kiss---will hold your future

Kind and noble; sweet and fun
    Always a smile
    Always my girl.
Mine to protect
    To nurture.

Now a Young Woman
    Beautiful eyes
    A smile like a sunrise
    Golden-souled

        Ambassador of Justice
            Of things that are Right.

Open Horizons meet you
> Like the fiery Sun hanging low
>> Near the calm winter's Ocean
>> Shimmering, blinding ripples of light everywhere—
>>> Repeating bursts of life with Promise.

Your world awaits you
> Like a red-tailed hawk sitting on the peak ready to fly-
>> Mountains of trees, a valley, a river, a lake, a road,
>>> A hidden path; sky, clouds.

BREATHE.
> I can't wait to see your flight!

Go forward and touch the world with your Golden-heart.

The journey is yours. It is time. Take it.
> You're ready. Don't Hesitate.

This is your story.

Write it.

Don't give in to worry. The Sun never has. Why should you?

Happily Ever After is here.

I said I love you and I meant it.

LaVan Robinson

LaVan Robinson writes in honor of his mother.

Robinson is a veteran and father. He has written poetry since high school. "LaLa" is his stage name. He uses poetry for inspiration. You can find LaLa performing at open mics and on podcasts. He can be found on social media.

Books by LaVan Robinson: *Songs of LaLa: The Poet - Second Edition, Love's Rhapsody, Cries of a Society - LaLa Speaks, Love's Anticipation-LaLa Seeks* (2020). He is currently working on a collaboration of poetry about hope.

In Thee

From the heavens above, it came pouring down upon my essence. For I was spiritually, mentally, and physically drained and so tired, so very tired and felt like I was about to expire. Just when it seemed I couldn't go much further and crawling on my knees was I. Unclear who and what it was I felt an entity by my side. Its presence bought about in me a surge of energy and strength I never before experienced. It picked me up from my knees and from there started my spiritual repentance. My essence was fully replenished and given a boundless source of hope. As my eyes cleared, I finally could see that it was the spirit of God that had come suddenly upon me. I quickly dropped back down to my knees in order to give it its due honor, praise, and blessings. Pleased was he that said to me now, my child, share this story among humanity because I'm now in thee.

Souls Beats

The rhythm of life is dictated by the beats of your soul. Within it is a precious treasure to receive and behold. You have the power to make your life lyrically sound. Adding to the orchestra of the essence that cannot be bound. Freely it's meant to flow, and others enlighten. Exposing the soul to the musical compositions that are meant to heighten.

True meaning of Life

Waking up hearing the birds outside my window jubilantly sing. They dare not worry about what the day will bring. They humbly go about their business knowing that God will provide their needs as we should know that our souls with his blessings he'll feed. Tomorrow isn't promise to no one but if you're blessed to see another day do appreciate the warmth from the rays of the sun. All your needs, trust God to provide for that's the true meaning of life.

Leslie Chartier

Leslie Chartier is a Chef and a writer with poetry in her soul and a future cookbook or two in her head. Her love of world travel fuels both her passion for cooking and for writing, as she shares her travel experiences with others through food and words. Leslie lives contentedly in Chatham County, NC with her husband of nearly twenty years.

Heart Beats

African Drums

I close my eyes,
My head lowers,
And I move -
Senses overtaken,
Spirit quickened
By the rhythm -

The rhythm moves...

Generations
Sunsets
Moons
passing, passing -

The rhythm moves...

Whisper of grass
Caress of sun
Stamp of feet
Trill of tongue -
The rhythm moves...

Eden's daughter -
I am begun.

Cold Feet

What would you do if you were to find
My heart was as black
as an abandoned coal mine?
Would you toss me away so the crows I so hate
could pick meat off my bones -
Would you choose death as my fate?

What if you were to find you didn't want me no more
Would you kick my behind,
Would you show me the door?

Or would you stay
Would you suffer
Would you nobly stick it out?

Could you crack a weary smile
as you watched me scream and shout?

Could you tell me that you love me
After twenty years or more?
Would you kiss my face every morning,
Or would you wish for life... before?

Well, honey let me tell you
as I'm walking down this aisle
There are many, many questions behind
this wary smile.

Heart Beats

But in faith -I'll swallow doubt.
We'll try our hand at marital bliss.
I will do my best to trust you.
And you -
Seal it -- with a kiss.

Rain

softly drops on my window pane
And I glance, then stare
out my window.

At the drops, then through -
Until all is blurred.
A melancholy longing
stirs my heart's memory.

Running through the rain -
Alone
so young, so insecure

Leaves of brilliant orange
muted by the gray in the sky
and in my mind.

Lying bundled on the couch
inhaling a book,
Escaping pain through the pages
as the rain beat down.

Running,
Reading
because I could

Lonely,
Yearning,
because I was.

Heart Beats

Now the sun shines
I need escape no more,
The yearning fulfilled.

Now on those days when it rains,
my eyes still see the gray,
but peace
has swallowed pain.

Lucy Brummett

Lucy Brummett is a North Carolina writer and inspirational coach. She is on a mission to guide women to pursue their dreams and goals one step at a time.

Holding On

How I yearn to turn back time
Back to the things that once were
When times were simple
Without adornments or trinkets
Instead, when we roamed free
With our imagination
That took us to far and away places
Where time stood still
In its innocence and wonder
We inhaled the times of youth
No longer yesterday
To be replaced with the passing
Of time spent
Reminiscing of the things
That once were
Now embedded in the crevices
Of our hearts

All Wrapped Up

So much thought for a gift
Meant for someone that you
Hold dear to your heart
That makes it flutter
Just so in a way
That only a special person
Can make you feel
As if you're the only one
In the room
Filled with noise and good cheer
Yet their love silences
All that for a moment
Where you feel like
You're the only one
On a pedestal
Taking their breath away

Surrender

A babbling brook calms my soul
It whispers to me softly
In a way that comforts
Like sunshine on a summer day
Enveloping me in a warmth
That penetrates down to my bones
Radiating a happiness
So serene with its touch
I close my eyes
To think about what is
On the other side
Of that bridge
A different path
That is unknown
Yet it beckons me
With an outstretched hand
To go towards it
With childlike curiosity

marisela brazfield

mb was born and raised in urban Los Angeles and is a Gen X'er who chronicles and scrawls about the art form of living in the Angelino metropolitan environment these offerings are inspired by the mental health crisis in the city, everyday observations, and human nature interjected with fiction based on non-fictional events.

Valentina

little Valentina jumped up and down by the crosswalk waiting for the light to turn lime jello green her little black patent leather shoes tip tapped on the dirty dusty sidewalk she let go of her mom's hand to clean the dust off open little palms were no match for the dirt those were her prized church doctor and special school event shoes they couldn't get dirty Valentina had an excellent day at the dentist and her mom and dad promised her she could go to Olvera Street and get her treat as the family made their way to the Plaza Valentina's eyes search like a hawk she didn't see Don Chema the paleta man with his cart filled with frozen delights it was a humble little ice box covered with ice pop stickers shaped like action heroes Sponge Bob and even the Disney Princesses once they got to the kiosk and the giant tree Valentina's hopes dimmed she looked up at her dad with the biggest brownest sullen eyes and he offered a dreadful solution would you like a churro instead Valentina searched once more and as a small crowd of Japanese tourists dispersed she saw Don Chema she hopped and squealed with delight Valentina pulled on her parents to walk her to the paletero Don Chema in a nasally raspy voice asked her que le gustaria mi reina Valentina whispered up to her dad and she asked for the prized watermelon paleta juicy red with the little black seeds frozen inside

Marjorie Maddox

Professor of English at Lock Haven University, Marjorie Maddox has published 11 collections of poetry—including *Transplant, Transport, Transubstantiation* (Yellowglen Prize)—the story collection *What She Was Saying* (Fomite); 4 children's and YA books—including *Inside Out: Poems on Writing and Reading Poems with Insider Exercises*—and *Common Wealth: Contemporary Poets* on Pennsylvania (co-editor). Forthcoming in 2021 are *Begin with a Question* (Paraclete) and *Heart Speaks, Is Spoken For* (Shanti Arts). Please see www.marjoriemaddox.com in 2021. For more information, please see marjoriemaddox.com

Transplanted

Though they'd never met,
the man with the dead man's heart
inside him dreamed his donor's
face, limbs, lungs; sung in his sleep
the dead man's favorite song
in the deep baritone voice
that wasn't his own but
his, the one not known or seen or heard,
except in night's deep cradle of sleep,
this stranger's metronome of a heart
humming behind ribs that no longer
felt like his—beautiful fence
for an organ lifted from someone else's
afterlife. Even waking, the new-
old man and his heart now know
nothing of old boundaries, the ones
composed by the living. Instead,
in bright, silent daylight,
he takes his first,
tentative beat
toward love.

Heart Beats

Ode to Almost-Silence

Praise to the door clicking shut,
to absence warming up the room,

but not completely: fireplace flame still
spitting its lazy opinions, radiator

humming its calm, the floorboard's creak
letting you know it's still there

but won't interrupt like the brash
morning jazz your husband plays

before coffee opens the ears
to thought and conversation.

Here: the louder hush of outside world
kept out—wind, occasional cat,

an emergency (not yours)
begging for someone else
to run, or fix, or bark commands
that can't break into this cordoned-off

zone of chosen contemplation—
where, sometimes, even now, you hear

Heart Beats

the memory of waves, the scratch
of sole on sand, the swirl of shells, and even

your chin lifting into salty air
as you listen not for the lost

and gone, but for what is
there and here inside

the ear and the empty
house, not empty after all.

Heart Beats

Inside

One house and this rhythm of ritual:
6:00 am, 8:00 am, 4:00 pm—our laptops open
in the kitchen, the living room, a bedroom,
Hellos at the refrigerator, while ascending/
descending the stairs, the constant tap of keys
the background of faraway horses we're all riding—
professor/parents, one-day professor/son—
across this long expanse of knowledge where we're
kicking up dust *someone goes out for a walk;*
someone returns on our way to a strange horizon
we hope is sunrise. *Good morning.*
Good afternoon. Good night. And we gather
for whatever's unfrozen or freshly baked,
and we watch what makes us laugh or tear up
or say *Proud of you. Love you. Thank you.*
And one stays up all night writing essays.
And two wake up early grading essays.

And everywhere there is typing and Zoom.
And on the morning and the evening
of the two-hundredth day, there is much darkness,
but also light. And it was good.
It was still good.

Maya Dykstra

Maya Dykstra is a Sophomore student at the University of Nebraska at Omaha. She is currently studying Studio Art with a concentration in Graphic Design and a minor in Creative Writing. She has made academics her number one priority with maintaining a 4.0 GPA. At the age of 17, Maya wrote and self-published her first novel. Since then, she has been published several times in *Fine Lines*, a Creative Writing Journal organization. When she isn't reading or writing, she is spending time with her younger sisters and supportive parents. Recently, she has become a leader as the New Members Director within her sorority. She is a well-rounded individual who lives with passion, creativity, and determination.

Theater Dreams

Velvet fabric meets a silky skirt,
Her date flats the wrinkles in his dress shirt.
A pair of eyes wonder across the crowd,
While a heart beats wildly like a storm cloud.

Hands link together upon her nervous thigh,
The front section was pricey, so they sat high.
Few people line the aisles among the couple,
Darkness awakes causing the light to struggle.

A lump of anticipation settles in her throat,
While tiny hairs stand waiting for the first note.
The tailored man takes his post with a stick,
As it strikes, rows of bows stand quick.

Shadows slowly melt away into the cracks,
As the spotlights begin the dance into the climax.
Strings craft a haunting melody with its cries,
Her spirit awakens, stretching towards the skies.

Heart Beats

Chilling bumps bloom across her smooth arms,
Enchanted is her heart within the song's charms.
Eyes of hopeful wishes overflow onto her lap,
The crowd stands as she gets lost in the claps.

Walking out of the room once filled with song,
The woman smiles as she sings her way along.

Heart Beats

In My World

Petals fall behind planting in my footsteps,
Laughter leads the way into the trees.
As the nectarine sun sets, I accept,
The moon will rise when I say please.

Tiny helicopter seeds fall like broken fairies,
Little frogs leap beside me on the pathway.
My fingers reach for the branch full of cherries,
Bright red lips whisper goodbye to the day.

Chasing shooting stars in the depth of the dark,
Lungs welcome nature's chilling breeze.
Fireflies argue with the constellations causing a spark,
The moon's shape is a noodle of macaroni and cheese.

Morning dew crystallizes as the sleep settles in,
Lemon sunshine of pure joy rises in the valley.
The tickling grass and the lily's waltz begin,
For this is the beginning, not the finale.

Ever Growing, Ever Healing

Ticks of the clock move me along,
Harmonizing with my keyboard in song.
Words appear like forgotten ghost of the past,
Sentences line the pages intending to last.

I've met females that will never exist,
Created their lover that they have kissed.
Killed off friends that meant so much to them,
Painful tears that destroyed them until they went numb.

Fresh white pages glow on my screen,
I own the blank page like a storytelling queen.
My subjects are my eager readers seeking the plot,
The twist I will write will hit hard in the blind spot.

No one but I will know what it's like,
Lightning behind my words will strike.
I cannot describe the welcoming feeling,
But it is in my soul, ever growing, ever healing.

Michael Murdoch

Born beneath the Southern Cross, Michael Murdoch a.k.a. the mouse, is a poet and fiction writer, who chased love to his new home under the Northern Lights.

He resides in Helsinki with his wife and three children.

You can find a selection of his works at his home away from home, *The Twisting Tail*.

Affirmations (I Wish My Words were Good Enough)

I know my silly words

aren't good enough to convince you

But that doesn't mean I won't try

The truth is

There's

No one like you

And there never will be

again

A piece of you

Is in every heart you've met

When you go

That piece goes with you

And creates a hole

in each heart left behind

Heart Beats

No matter what
or how you feel
You are never alone
Someone feels just like you

Your soul is a gift
More valuable than anything on earth
Stronger than any suffering
Don't give it away

A Single Smile

A single smile
can change the world
I know
Because your smile
changed mine

I knew then
In that first
moment
I was lost
Forever

Lost
To the world
We knew before

Now
Years later
We are together
Finding the way
In our own little world

Nayanjyoti Baruah

Nayanjyoti Baruah is from Assam, India. He is pursuing an M. A. in English Literature from Gauhati University. He has written about 115 poems both in English and in his mother tongue (Assamese). His poems have appeared in *Tayls, Rasa Literary Review, Felicity, The Fiction Project, A Too Powerful Word, Necro Magazine*, and more. He is the Co-author of *"The Bag of Knowledge"* and *"Being an Indian Teenager,* awaiting publication. He has written two essays and four short stories.

Happiness

Here and there happiness is,
But no one recognizes where it is.
Every day everyone runs after it, but
Almost everyone knows not what it is.
Happiness is found high and low;
But it's not goods to go and purchase from the store.
One great outlook requires for
Seeing, smelling, feeling, and finding it.
Farmers smell it in the paddy field,
Rickshaw men find it in the full passenger's seat,
Pregnant women feel it after giving birth to a baby,
When wage labors always get paid in the evening.
Let's surrender ourselves at our work,
And struggle to achieve it, score it.
Let us steal not others' happiness
Until we deserve it.

O My Disease Beloved

O my disease beloved, as I hath to thee,
I couldn't behold thy symptoms of sameness.
I scan thy ever-burning eyes that captured my portrait,
Unfortunately, I couldn't see any positive sign.
Didst ye recall when I checked thy soft body intentionally?
That thy high temperature warmed pulse?
Where didst thee cut off that connecting cord?
Let's not spread thy symptoms to others,
Let it confine to only between thee and me.
Thee must acknowledge our last touching,
Indirectly I manifested everything before thee.
Thee didst not see anything, not even know why?
Now thou art a different person that I loved once.
I doth not feel the same touch, but a new symptom of love.

We Shall be an Example of Love.

She is busy with a cigarette in between red lips,
Goblet in one hand when I have seen her.
I am too busy flirting with girls.
Her loaded, magnet, chilly figure
Tells all what I am waiting for.
And I've sunk in ocean of attraction with her.
We teenagers,
Take not an archetypal step, rather
Let us make our love as an example of love
For our coming teenagers.
We are not an artist of perfection,
Nor we are students for being concentrated,
We are like tsunami,
Like an infant ready for having drink,
We are new, let us enjoy our warmth figure.
O Director of the Cosmos, teach me how do I love?
Let's entwine our body,
You try to forget everything and lie on me.

Heart Beats

Since our long intimacy have completed,
We should not wait for discussion!
Before we depart and continue our lives
As nothing has happened to us,
How can I forget to ask
Tell me what is your name at first?

Norbert Góra

Norbert Góra is a 30-year-old poet and writer from Poland. He is the author of more than 100 poems which have been published in poetry anthologies in USA, UK, India, Nigeria, Kenya, and Australia.

Transmission of love

Love is like a stream,
a transmitter of emotions
that lets the heart beat.

Heartbeat accelerator

I am a poet,
nothing fuels the heart more than
the charm of poems.

The heart beats for challenges

Life is a set of
challenges that must be faced,
incessant heartbeat.

Peniel Gifted

Peniel Gifted is a young Nigerian poet and writer. She has great enthusiasm for reading, writing, and learning and also an adroit lover of nature and God's word.

Like A Rainbow

Like a rainbow
Olio of simpering dream
Blinks in the lid.

Dream of offing
Laced with candied
Brown and white.

Blooming-
Our crinum, nursed when
The blinders were ruddy.

Wiggling-
The cloverleaves
Of our clock and circle.

Through Our World

Through our world
Of wild dreams that bloom
Like china pink-rejuvenating.

Painted in deep
Oceans of Canaan
And blithe in Disa's beauty.

Palaces in azalea's gown
With manifold chivalry
Each locus-abode of blue banderole.

Millennium of Amorpha's flurry
Millennium of sweet peeps' melody
Millennium of mounting and athletic emmets.

Richard O. Ogunmodede

Richard O. Ogunmodede is a Nigerian. He is a poet and an author; he has co-authored a poetry book and he's also into short story writing. He's an artisan, a husband, and a father of three lovely kids and he is based in Nigeria. He loves playing board games such as chess, Scrabble, and Monopoly.

Heart Beats

When the Poets are Long Gone

Bring back the memories of my lovely genre
It's not from the armory but his diary
Oh! words could be more precious than big-ticket

I wondered around bookstores,
Couldn't find a copy left aside that in his diary
His lyrics were expensive
But the pen that inked them was less
The wise few couldn't help but reference his words
And men who seek knowledge, hunt for his works
Placing his diary for the print of inks, will
Bring back the value of what we seem to have lost
The gracious moment that gives me joy is knowing,
Poetic words can be immortalized, if well-inked,
Let the Heavens bless the inks left behind by departed poets

Heart Beats

We are Same

My heart beats just like yours'
If it stops, I would be gone
My blood is red, just like yours'
If it's blue, then I'm what?
We share the same image, such as God's
Though the colors differ, that shouldn't matter
When the sun rises over my head,
It sets over yours',
To change turn for another day,
Nature hasn't been partial
Here's my hand, grip it firm,
Touch my heart, fill the beat,
Allow my lips to wipe your tears,
We could trek safely through the earthy path,
As each other's keeper

Richard Oyama

Richard Oyama's work has appeared in *Premonitions: The Kaya Anthology of New Asian North American Poetry*, *The Nuyorasian Anthology*, *Breaking Silence*, *Dissident Song*, *A Gift of Tongues*, *About Place*, *Konch Magazine*, *Pirene's Fountain*, *Tribes*, *Malpais Review*, *Anak Sastra* and other literary journals. *The Country They Know* (Neuma Books 2005) is his first collection of poetry. He has a M.A. in English: Creative Writing from San Francisco State University. Oyama taught at California College of Arts in Oakland, University of California at Berkeley, and University of New Mexico. His first novel in a trilogy, *A Riot Goin' On*, is forthcoming.

Heart Beats

My Heart

For poetry makes nothing happen . . .
A way of happening, a mouth.
   --W.H. Auden

My heart is isinglass and steel. It
Slakes your thirst and is sweet.
You part your lips. My heart flows out to you
Like a song or poem. It sings praise.
It is inside you now—your tongue, throat.
My cartoon heart is in your mouth,
A dark wood of witchy trees where everything is
As transparent and pellucid as Waterford,
Thin and chipped. It is
Blown glass with an apex that can be
Eaten like a wafer. My heart is
A golden bowl swimming with fish.

For SLK

Kind

n. a group with similar characteristics, or a particular type

The women who embody virtues I revere,
   These pilgrims in their unstoppable progress,
And the men, escaping our armor,
Making life a commedia, an art,
   Breaking the masculine code.
They are all the things I have ever cherished
   And in this allegory, they are walking the earth.
We must prize them for they are our Fate.
I cannot talk of she who calls me a Pokemon, rare creature,
Or she who has the yogic energies of equability.
They possess the gift of recognition and subtle mind.
If the ones I loved passed into that pure moment of death,
   They find local habitation in these youth who
     Raise the future like a sacrament.

Delusioner

For Matthew J. Wells

Invisible Man meets Portnoy, the blurb raves.

My property would be a multi-book deal, exclusive cable rights,

Translation into 26 languages, Bridget Jones hosting the launch,

Airport racks chock-a-block.

On *Shinkansen* and D train, every passenger

A-swim in my masterpiece—

Brilliant mash-up of Shakespeare & Pryor. I close on

A Bel-Air mansion and don't give out the address.

My new friends are gorgeous in

The exact same way. We lounge around the pool, talking

High concept and weekend grosses.

Mazzy Star's on the box: dream-pop for end-times.

Ronda M. Smith

Ronda M. Smith had her first poem published at age 7. She is a writer, world traveler, creative problem solver, entrepreneur, innovator, developer of leaders, industrial/organizational psychologist, mother, and a home school teacher. She earns her living as an Assistant Professor of Management and has a hard time sitting still.

Patience in the Moment

It stopped for a moment - But it felt more like years.
Realizing what happened - All he had was tears.

He looked over at her, such a small little one.
How could life be over before it had begun?

When the moment had passed, He heard it again!
The tears they kept falling. It's not really the end!

Her little heart beat strong in her chest.
It seems just for the moment, it needed to rest.

A long life ahead, but a strong memory they made.
Patience in the moment.
Joy, for the rest of her days!

Sarfraz Ahmed

Sarfraz Ahmed lives and works in East Midlands, UK, and is a careers adviser, branching out as trainer, assessor, and a careers writer. He has been writing poetry for over eighteen years and has contributed to many anthologies, including *Paint the Sky with Stars*, published by Re-invention UK and many others published by the United Press, and many online contributions. His published books include poetry debut *Eighty-Four Pins* (June 2020) and *My Teachers an Alien!* (November 2020) which is a children's book with illustrator Natasha Adams. Green Cat Books. published both books https://green-cat.co/books He has published his second collection of poetry, along with Annette Tarpley, *Two Hearts* (February 2021). Sarfraz moderates the large Passion of Poetry group on Facebook and has a following on Facebook and Instagram. We can find him at open mic events, has shared his poetry globally, including the New York circuit.

The Virus That Kills

The green grass rolls over the hills,
A multitude of colours sparkle and spill,
Whisper through shades of magnolia,
Through blossoms of white,
As butterflies flutter and intertwine,
In the glorious sunshine,

Flowers are in full bloom,
Dressed up with nowhere to go,
They wear their bonnets and hats,
And put on a show,

They greet each other,
Bow their heads to and fro,
As they gently begin to turn to the sun,
In the early morning dew,

But if only,
They were to turn their heads,
The other way,
If only they knew,

Heart Beats

The darkness that dwells
Softly polluting the heavens,
Crumbling humanity,
Incubating a living hell,

But I don't think the flowers know,
I don't think they really care,
That the virus is spreading,
That it is everywhere,

Through the glass,
I watch the butterflies,
Flutter and intertwine,
In the glorious heat,
In the sunshine,

The green grass continues to roll over the hills,
A multitude of colours sparkle and spill,
As we all hide in self-isolation,
From the virus that kills,

Estate (Summer)

The sun kissed all the blue,
The hot Mediterranean sun glistened,
Melts down on all of you,
As you slip and slide,
You take my hand,
You hold it tight,
As we walk across the golden sand,

It envelops and folds,
Covers us up in all that's gold,
The hot summer rays sparkles and shines,
Intertwine in between the palm trees,
As the cool summer breeze whispers,
Gently over the majestic scene,
We both look at each other,
And delve into the dream.

Sheila DC Robertson

In the barren landscapes that define southwestern Idaho, Sheila DC Robertson seeks beauty and stories off the beaten path. With pen and camera, she is happiest in the deep winding canyons of the Owyhee or camped out under the stars in its remotest weathered desert.

With the inspiration of her husband and two children, she has published poetry, articles, and short stories.

Frames

Rising before dawn
   I stalk the light
   As it arrives
   Cold and hungry

I frame and focus
Press the shutter release
Capture morning's glide
   Gray to golden

Standing in frosted fields
   I live behind a focal plane
   Fuse with images
   Caught in a viewfinder

I slide along a flyline's arc
   Dancing over autumn water
   Bright caddis fly sparkling
   Above the trout's rise

Heart Beats

Beard's spike from heads of grain
Ice crystal facets on snow meadows
I freeze these moments
   In the flow of time

The lens of my Nikon crops out
   The grainy terrors
   Of threatening words
   And trampled dreams

It stops down
   Larger worlds gone mad
   Blood stains on streets
   Hungry eyes and mass migrations

I follow a focus
   That tugs me along curving stamens
   Into the lime green throat
   Of a cactus flower

Open up to a kingfisher's wing
   A glinting blue up-beat
   Just before the dive
   When soul holds hands with the eye

Heart Beats

Across sun-limned clouds
   The twisting dance of mating eagles
   And the catch of my heart
   Are captured together

I live in the moment and ride
   Planes of light
   So achingly beautiful
   That I must possess them

Where my frame of mind
   And frame of view
   Merge in patterns
   Of sanity

That hold me tight
   When pixelating frames
   Of the world
   Are flying apart

Flight

In my jewelry box
   there is an unlikely necklace
   for a grandmother of a certain age
It lies next to a string of pearls

To you it may look like a gray river stone
   perhaps in the shape of a raptor's head

Through the smooth natural hole of the eye
   passes a leather thong
   knotted and tied with tiny brass bells
   the kind used on hawks' jesses

To me
   it possesses magic

As I lift it from the velvet lining
   the smell of the leather
   the shape of the stone
   and the tinkling of bells

Take me to windy hilltops
   flying falcons.

Imagined Intents

Blades bristle and cross
Doing battle in my garden
Purple flags face yellow pennants
Waving in ranks
Until I come snipping
Among their armies
With scissors and vase
Discard my imagined intent
To grace my kitchen table

Sreekala P Vijayan

Sreekala P Vijayan is a prolific writer. She is an academician by profession. Her poems resonate every person of its kind. Her ink is a complete blend of all varieties- art, environment, pleasure, love, hope and so on. Her works reveals her inner strength, addressing the narratives of human experiences.

Papa's girl.

Featherlite she flew, across the greens,
Dewdrops on her little toes, kissed with all its glow.
Euphoric speculations, thrilled her,
Her face registered surfacing of joy.
Tender pinky fingers, lulled the frondescence,
Two luminous pearls luxuriate the blossoms.
Chubbiness of her cheeks,
Was waiting for the love filled pull,
Dimples to hypnotise the hearts.

She is Papa's girl, prettiest doll,
Fluttered around to sit on his lap.
Amazing love,
Daughter to her father,
Heartwarming sight to witness

© Sreekala P Vijayan

Susi Bocks

Susi Bocks, writer/author/poet, has self-published two books - *Feeling Human* and *Every Day I Pause* and is the Editor of *The Short of It*. You can find her work at IWriteHer.com where she invites you to read her thoughts to get to know her or follow, *I Write Her* on Facebook. Bocks' work has been published in the *anthologies As the World Burns, SMITTEN: This Is What Love Looks Like: Poetry by Women for Women* and in *VitaBrevis, Spillwords, Literary Yard*, and other literary magazines.

Sweet Embrace

even though life burdens us with chronic ills-
unfortunate, inconvenient, and untimely

they are all these

but regardless of diminishing delights, despite the looming fear

our wants still long for self-determined joy

parents, grandmothers, grandfathers, close friends, lovers, children

and the cultural norms of some countries laid aside

we demand what once was so common, that which we've side-lined out of concern

and care for the living and vulnerable

while we slowly readjust to a new reality, creativity forces our hand

determined to fill the wants that now have become needs

saving us from further despair, no more taking hits to our equilibrium

as the plastic curtain crinkles in the arms of who we love

A New Life

with what started as a joyous event
this dampening year interfered in the emotions
it burst bubbles and created hesitation
normal anxieties on top of other worries now
the natural cycle of life shifts to new concerns

make the best of it, they say

the stirrings of a new life remind us heightened
    expectations
remain in our purview, and rightly so
as we gaze into the eyes of a blended intention
hope and joy are restored
with each gurgle, coo, and smile

Heart Beats

Raucous

humor grips tightly
at the end of a rough year
belly laughs explode

Vandana Sudheesh

Vandana Sudheesh was born in Kozhikode district in the southern Indian state of Kerala. She started writing under the influence of world-famous writers from an early age. She has completed MBA and worked for Axis Bank Limited in India and later went to Early Retirement. She then devoted herself to composing poetry. She is a moderator of Motivational Strips and directs Asian writers through a parliamentary committee of forum members. Considering his passion, enthusiasm, and contribution to world literature, he was awarded membership of the World Nation Writers Union (WNWU). Her solo book *The Humble Wrath* has been published. To date, his poems have been written in four collections of poetry, *Poets Unify World, A Gift- III, Pastel Shades of Love* and *Crescent Moon*. She is also a regular contributor to Indian newspapers and magazines. He is also a regular contributor to *Web Magazine* and Social Media. Notable among these are *Dhoni* and *Irreplaceable Legend, Aroma of Notion, Bharat Vision, etc.* published by Oxigle Press. Apart from writing, she is also a dancer, an artist and singer.

Let's Hop and Dance

Let's hop and dance in the shores of forgiveness
A gesture of accepting the mistakes with smile
Let's get drenched in the light of the morning star
To start a new day fresh and blessed with hope

Give me your hand I will take care of you
No matter what happens I stay by your side
Never fear stumbling upon the stones of ignorance
I am there forever to support your existence

Sing aloud the song of pride for the endless energy
I will tap my feet one two three along with you
You feel your conscience smiling within your eyes
Let 'them'(others)mutter the words of benevolence

Our wish to laugh and cry no room for a third face to rotten
Make time to sit and talk until the night has fallen
No money is worth what we had shared deeply
Wear a smile to turn off the rumbling noise

Hear your heart beating to your beloved one
Never waste time to see things adversely
Because one life is all we have to remember
Let's make it a celebration each day with love and care

©□Vandana Sudheesh

Lisa Tomey

Lisa Tomey, Member & Manager of Prolific Pulse Press LLC, wears many hats. With a love of reading poetry as a young child, along with creating with ideas from a Junior Instructor book, she grew with her love of the creative process. Bitten by the poetry writing bug in grade school, she was first published- along with her sixth-grade class-in an anthology of Asian forms of poetry. After that, there was no looking back. Since that time, she has published a poetry chapbook Heart Sounds, and has been published in numerous journals, including *Fine Lines*, of which she is a member of the editorial staff.

You can find her at ProlificPulse.com and blogging at ProlificPulse.blog

Heart Beats

This is Not a Poem

This is not a poem
from the moment I lay in the warmth of her womb
protected from the world--I felt her love
the songs she sang and the way she walked
carrying me within I knew I was loved
This is not a poem
but an anthem of sorts
When I entered the world
the air touched my face and I cried
she was the first to hear
this is not a poem
it's a record one could say
mom used to tell the story
of my birth day every birthday
of how she counted my fingers and toes
and I was her beautiful child
this is not a poem
it is the closeness of my mother's heart
and the iambic pentameter
of her heartbeat

Thank you for reading this collection of poetry from many poets from around the world.

Stay safe and keep well and may you be blessed always.

Heart Beats - Anthology of Poetry

Heart Beats

Heart Beats

Made in the USA
Monee, IL
06 April 2021